Super Chef

THE COOKING OF
India

MATTHEW LOCRICCHIO

WITH PHOTOS BY

JACK MCCONNELL

BENCHMARK BOOKS

MARSHALL CAVENDISH
NEW YORK

This book is dedicated to my brother Pandu.

ACKNOWLEDGMENTS

Cookbooks require dedication and teamwork, and I am very lucky to be supported by individuals who display both. My sincere gratitude goes to the members of the Superchef Recipe Testers Club and their adult assistant chefs whose testing, comments, and suggestions are invaluable: Saun Ellis and Sonia Drojohowska of Sherman, Connecticut; and Vicki Navratil and Kayla and Steven Kosovac of Hudson, New York. I am also very grateful to Kathie Lewis of Grosse Pointe, Michigan, Brenda Scamuzzi, Robert and Marsha Hall, Jane Rainwater, Saundra Dring, Linda Harmon, and Cosmos International Market. I am particularly grateful to Aid to Artisans of Hartford, Connecticut, for loaning us the beautiful fabrics, created by Indian craftspeople, used in our recipe photos. Thanks also go to Chobi Choudhury of New Milford, Connecticut, for her generous time in teaching me some of the basics of Indian cooking, and Sudeb Bose of Calcutta for his help. As always my thanks go to the enduring Dr. Archie Karfly, whose unwavering help and support were essential in creating this book.

Benchmark Books
Marshall Cavendish
99 White Plains Road
Tarrytown, New York 10591-9001
www.marshallcavendish.us

Text copyright © 2005 by Matthew Locricchio
Food photographs © 2005 Jack McConnell, McConnell, McNamara & Company
Art director for food photography: Matthew Locricchio
Map copyright © 2005 by Mike Reagan

Illustrations by Janet Hamlin
Illustrations copyright © 2005 by Marshall Cavendish Corporation

Series design by Anahid Hamparian
Food styling by Marie Hirschfeld and Matthew Locricchio

Library of Congress Cataloging-in-Publication Data

Locricchio, Matthew.
  The cooking of
India / by Matthew Locricchio.
     p. cm. — (Superchef)
Includes index.
Summary: Introduces the different culinary regions of India through
recipes adapted for young chefs and discusses the basics of food
handling and kitchen safety.
ISBN 0-7614-1730-3
1. Cookery, Indic. [1. Cookery, Indic. 2. Food habits—India.] I.
Title. II. Series.

TX724.5.I4L63 2003
641.5954—dc22
2003014916
Photo research by Rose Corbett Gordon, Mystic, CT
Photo credits: Michael Freeman/Corbis:12; Nicholas DeVore/Getty Images:14.

Printed in Italy
    3   5   6   4   2

Contents

DEAR READER,

I WILL ALWAYS REMEMBER THE AROMA OF ONIONS, CELERY, AND BELL PEPPER COOKING IN MY MOTHER'S CAST-IRON DUTCH OVEN. THAT APPETIZING AROMA PERMEATES MY CHILDHOOD MEMORIES AS IT DID OUR HOME. ONE OF THE MOST DELIGHTFUL THINGS I HAVE LEARNED AS A CHEF IS HOW DEEPLY FOOD INFLUENCES OUR LIVES. FOOD TOUCHES PEOPLE ON SO MANY LEVELS—PHYSICALLY, EMOTIONALLY, SOCIALLY, AND SPIRITUALLY. THE PUBLIC'S INTEREST IN FOOD AND CUISINE IS INSATIABLE, AND I AM CONSTANTLY AMAZED AT THE LEVEL OF INTEREST AND KNOWLEDGE I SEE IN YOUNG PEOPLE. THE CUISINES OF THE WORLD ARE WIDE AND VARIED AND GIVE US A GOOD PICTURE OF HUMAN NATURE AT ITS BEST. A STUDY OF THE WORLD'S MANY DIFFERENT CUISINES UNVEILS THE RICH TAPESTRY OF CULTURAL DIFFERENCES, YET IN THE END WE LEARN ONE OF LIFE'S MOST VALUABLE LESSONS: FOOD BRINGS PEOPLE TOGETHER.

THESE COOKBOOKS, WHICH I HEARTILY ENDORSE, GIVE YOUNG PEOPLE THE CHANCE TO EXPLORE, TO CREATE, AND TO LEARN. IN **Superchef**, YOUNG READERS CAN USE THEIR HOME KITCHENS TO EXPLORE THE MANY DIFFERENT TASTES OF THE WORLD. THEY CAN LEARN THE VALUE OF WORKING TOGETHER WITH FAMILY MEMBERS IN THE HOME AND EXPERIENCE THE SHEER PLEASURE OF A PERFECT MEAL. WHEN THE CUTTING, CHOPPING, AND COOKING ARE OVER, IT'S TIME TO SIT DOWN TOGETHER AND ENJOY THE FRUITS OF THE ASPIRING CHEF'S LABOR. THIS IS WHEN YOUNG CHEFS CAN LEARN THE **REAL** SECRET OF THE GREAT CHEFS—THE JOY OF SHARING.

CHEF FRANK BRIGTSEN

BRIGTSEN'S RESTAURANT
NEW ORLEANS, LOUISIANA

From the Author

Welcome to **Superchef**. This series of cookbooks brings you traditional recipes from other countries, adapted to work in your kitchen. My goal is to introduce you to a world of exciting and satisfying recipes, along with the basic principles of kitchen safety, food handling, and common-sense nutrition. Inside you will find classic recipes from India. The recipes are not necessarily all low-fat or low-calorie, but they are all healthful. Even if you are a vegetarian, you will find recipes without meat or with suggestions to make the dish meatless.

Many people today eat lots of fast food and processed or convenience foods because they are "quick and easy." As a result there are many people both young and old who simply don't know how to cook and have never experienced the pleasure of preparing a successful meal. **Superchef** can change the way you feel about cooking. You can learn to make authentic and delicious dishes from recipes that have been tested by young cooks in kitchens like yours. The recipes range from very basic to challenging. The instructions take you through the preparation of each dish step by step. Once you learn the basic techniques of the recipes, you will understand the principles of cooking fresh food successfully.

There is no better way to get to know people than to share a meal with them. Today, more than ever, it is essential to understand the many cultures that inhabit our planet. One way to really learn about a country is to know how its food tastes. You'll also be discovering the people of other countries while learning to prepare their classic recipes.

Learning to cook takes practice, patience, and common sense, but it's not nuclear science. Cooking certainly has its rewards. Just the simple act of preparing food can lift your spirits. Nothing brings family and friends together better than cooking and then sharing the meal you made. It can be fun, and you get to eat your mistakes. It can even lead to a high-paying career. Most importantly, you can be proud to say, "Oh, glad you liked it. I did it myself."

See you in the kitchen!

Matthew Locricchio

Before You Begin

A WORD ABOUT SAFETY

Safety and common sense are the two most important ingredients in any recipe. Before you begin to make the recipes in this book, take a few minutes to master some simple kitchen safety rules.

✔ *Ask an adult to be your assistant chef. To ensure your safety, some steps in a recipe are best done with the help of an adult, like handling pots of boiling water or hot cooking oils. Good cooking is about teamwork. With an adult assistant to help, you've got the makings of a perfect team.*

✔ *Read the entire recipe before you start to prepare it, and have a clear understanding of how the recipe works. If something is not clear, ask your teammate to explain it.*

✔ *Dress the part of a chef. Wear an apron. Tie back long hair so that it's out of your food and away from open flames. Why not do what a chef does and wear a clean hat to cover your hair!*

✔ *Always start with clean hands and a clean kitchen before you begin any recipe. Leave the kitchen clean when you're done.*

✔ *Pot holders and hot pads are your friends. The hands they save may be your own. Use them only if they are dry. Using wet holders on a hot pot can cause a serious burn!*

✔ *Keep the handles of the pots and pans turned toward the middle of the stove. That way you won't accidentally hit them and knock over pots of hot food. Always use pot holders to open or move a pan on the stove or in the oven.*

✔ *Remember to turn off the stove and oven when you are finished cooking. Sounds like a simple idea, but it's easy to forget.*

Be Sharp about Knives

✔ *A simple rule about knife safety is that your hands work as a team. One hand grips the handle and operates the knife while the other guides the food you are cutting. The hand holding the food should never come close to the blade of the knife. Keep the fingertips that hold the food slightly curved and out of the path of the blade, and use your thumb to keep the food steady. Go slowly. There is no reason to chop very fast.*

✔ *Always hold the knife handle with **dry** hands. If your hands are wet, the knife might slip. Work on a cutting board, never a tabletop or countertop.*

✔ *Never place sharp knives in a sink full of soapy water, where they could be hidden from view. Someone reaching into the water might get hurt.*

✔ *Take good care of your knives. Good chef knives should be washed by hand, never in a dishwasher.*

Cooking Terms and Techniques

The unique tastes of Indian cooking come from blending the flavors of many ingredients into one. Indian food is created with more spices than perhaps any other national cuisine. The Indian cook knows how to achieve culinary magic by using the right balance of spices working in perfect harmony. Even though several different spices are often used, one particular flavor does not dominate the dish. Probably no other cuisine has produced cooks so skilled at using spice combinations, called *masalas,* so successfully.

Another key to great Indian cooking is using the freshest ingredients. When shopping for the dishes in this book, look for the freshest meats, seafood, and vegetables. Why not consider organic vegetables, fruits, poultry, or meats? Many people believe organic products taste better than nonorganic ones. They tend to be more expensive, though, so keep your budget in mind when you are shopping. Think of ingredients as the Indian cook does. Vibrant spices and appetizing high-quality ingredients are the essentials needed to achieve a culinary work of art.

Some people think that Indian dishes are just too spicy to eat. But Indian cooks are very skilled at adjusting the amount of "heat" in their recipes. You can do the same when you prepare your own dishes. Once you learn how to balance and blend the various spices, you will discover why the cooking of India has been popular for thousands of years. It takes plenty of patience and practice, and it isn't to be rushed. It takes time to prepare great Indian meals. Before you begin, be sure to organize and plan each recipe. The results will be worth the extra effort. Not only will you discover new spices and experience enticing aromas, you will also enjoy the pleasure of preparing and sharing real Indian cooking. Here are a few simple techniques to help you along as you follow the recipes in this book.

Grate   *To finely shred. A four-sided metal grater with a handle at the top will give you a place to hold on to as you work. Always use extreme caution when using a grater and don't allow your fingers to come too close to the grating surface.*

Sauté   *To lightly fry ingredients in a small amount of fat, butter, or oil, while stirring with a spoon or spatula. Onions are sautéed in a lot of Indian recipes to release their natural sugars. Once the sugar combines with the cooking oil, the onions turn golden and slightly crispy. When you sauté onions, it is important to keep stirring them to prevent them from burning or sticking.*

Simmer	*To cook food in a liquid kept just below the boiling point. Gentle bubbles will roll lazily to the top of a liquid that is simmering. Simmering is an important part of Indian cooking and is used to reduce or thicken sauces as well as to enrich flavor.*

Skim	*Fats or impurities rise to the surface of simmering or boiling soups and sauces. Skimming is a way to remove these unwanted residues both during cooking and before serving the dish. Use a large metal spoon or small ladle to scoop them gently from the surface of the liquid.*

Grinding Whole Spices If you are going to be doing any Indian cooking, it is important to have a way to grind whole spices. Although you can always buy spices already ground, you'll achieve the best flavor when you grind them fresh. The simplest way to grind whole spices is in an electric spice or coffee grinder. The important thing to remember about using a coffee grinder for your spices is that it must be used just for spices. You would never want to surprise the person using the grinder after you with a cup of coffee that ends up tasting like cumin or allspice. Once you grind the spices needed for a recipe, unplug the grinder and wipe it out with a damp paper towel and wash and dry the lid. That way the potent flavors won't linger and carry over to your next recipe. If you don't have an electric grinder, you can always use a common kitchen tool called a mortar and pestle. The mortar looks like a small bowl. It holds the spices that need to be crushed. The pestle is a club-shaped tool that has a rounded bottom. The pestle is used to pound and grind the spices in the bottom of the mortar into a fine powder.

From left to right: anise seeds, coriander, fennel, black mustard seeds, yellow mustard seeds, peppercorns, green cardamom, and cumin seeds.

The Regions of India and How They Taste

The cuisine of India, with its fragrant spices and diverse cultural and religious influences, has been thousands of years in the making. Family recipes have been handed down for generations, so often the best food is found not in restaurants, but in someone's home where sharing food is an expression of hospitality. When entering a family's home in India, you are likely to be offered something to eat as a way of welcoming you. It is regarded as rude to refuse it.

But the cooking of India and its impact extend far beyond the home. The history of Western civilization is tied to its spices. For centuries, explorers headed for India's shores to obtain the highly prized exotic spices. Along the way, they discovered new worlds and hastened the spread of ideas. Still it was securing the valuable spices that was one of their primary goals. Spices not only helped preserve food but also ultimately changed the cooking of the rest of the world. Slowly other cultures discovered that by adding spices foods became more flavorful, and the world's cuisines were never the same.

India is a large agricultural nation, marked by a diversity of regions, traditions, languages, and religions. This diversity has played a significant role in the development of its cooking. For simplicity, the nation will be divided into two main regions, the north and the south. Come along as we explore each and some of the tempting dishes made there.

THE NORTH

The long sweep of the Himalayas, the tallest and one of the youngest mountain ranges on the planet, separates India from China. This legendary chain, with its eternal, snow-crowned peaks, lush Kashmir Valley, and sparkling waterfalls, is certainly one of nature's masterpieces. It is through this beautiful valley that the nomadic Moghuls invaded India. The Moghuls ruled India for hundreds of years, and their culinary influence is evident today in the nation's cuisine.

Farms made up of small terraced plots of land dot the valley of Kashmir, where large orchards produce, among other things, apples, peaches, and pears. Sheep and goats graze on the steep hillsides and beside the groves of almond and walnut trees. Each year the nuts are harvested and pressed into cooking oils. But the most valuable crop to thrive there is the crocus. It produces saffron, the most expensive spice in world. It takes about 70,000 crocus flowers to produce 1 pound of saffron.

The people in the state of Kashmir are predominantly Muslim, so lamb plays an important role in their local recipes. The Kashmir cuisine is famous for its lamb

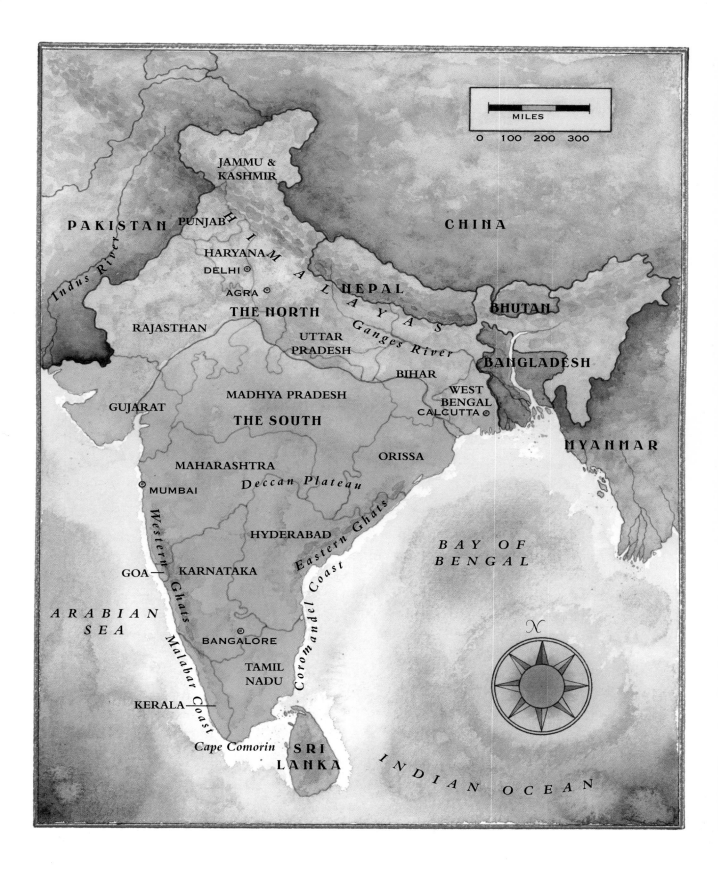

A regal elephant carries its proud rider through the streets of Jaipur.

stew, *rogan gosh,* a dish created with local yogurt, black cumin seeds, and a distinctive blend of spices. Another local recipe, a spicy marinated chicken with allspice, is often cooked over an open fire.

Just to the south of Kashmir is the state of Jammu. Both the Indus and Ganges rivers flow through this part of India, adding their precious waters to the region. Here the flat land and warm climate combine to create the ideal conditions for growing rice. An excellent long-grain rice called basmati is one of the area's major crops. It is regarded by many as the finest rice in the world.

To the south, along the Pakistan border, are the states of Punjab and Haryana with a combined population of more than 35 million people. A predominantly agricultural state, Punjab supplies about 50 percent of the nation's rice and more than 60 percent of its wheat. Vegetables such as eggplant, potatoes, a variety of legumes, and mustard plants grow in the fertile soils and find their way into many local recipes.

Royal rice, a recipe believed to be from the kitchens of the maharajas, or Hindu princes, combines spices and fresh vegetables into a dish that is as pleasing to the eye as it is to the taste buds. A sweetened, creamy rice dessert, called *kheer,* is popular throughout India. It is a specialty of the neighboring region of Haryana. Another regional favorite is chicken in a richly flavored gravy blended with fresh mint and yogurt. The Western term *curry* is probably taken from the Tamil word *kari. Kari* is a gravy or sauce that meats, seafood, or vegetables are cooked in along with a blend of spices.

Farther south lies Uttar Pradesh, where the sacred Ganges River continues along its course, flowing through a vast plain. Uttar Pradesh, which means "northern plain," is a massive expanse of land prone to flooding in the monsoon season. It is home to a combined population of more than 139 million people and has Delhi as its capital. Not far from Delhi is Agra, home to one of the world's most famous sites, the Taj Mahal.

The cuisine of the northern plain offers an amazing variety of dishes, especially vegetarian ones. The essential cooking fat of Uttar Pradesh is called *usli ghee,* which means, "real butter." But it is not the only form of cooking fat found here. The corn and mustard seeds grown in the region are pressed into other varieties of cooking oils as well and help supply the rest of India. Wheat, barley, potatoes, and sugarcane are also found here in abundance. The wheat is ground into flour and baked into flatbreads called *chapati,* which are made fresh for each meal. One specialty of the region is chicken and saffron-flavored rice baked together to create a dish called *biryani.* It is served on special occasions and is one of India's most adored recipes.

Travel to the western edge of Uttar Pradesh near the Pakistan border and you will discover Rajasthan, the Land of the Kings. Its capital city of Jaipur is vibrant and rich with Indian history and tradition. Many of the local men dress in colorful garments and silken turbans. The houses in the old city, many of which are pink, date back to the tenth century. Camels, which carry fresh vegetables and fruit for sale through the streets, are important not only to the city but the entire region. Each year hundreds of thousands of visitors come to the little town of Pushkar. They bring nearly fifty thousand camels with them to take part in, what else, a festival of camels! Cookies called *ladoos* are sold on the streets along with many other local delicacies to mark this spectacular celebration.

Gujarat, just south of Rajasthan, produces, among other things, a wealth of sugarcane. This may explain why the local cooks are famous for sweet vegetable dishes. Buttery spinach, made with cashews, sweet currants, sugar, and chiles, is just one irresistible example.

To the east along the Bangladesh border is the state of West Bengal. It is a region of amazing cultural diversity, fertile plains, and outstanding cuisine. Its capital, Calcutta, is the country's second-largest city. It is widely regarded as the nation's cultural center as many of India's most esteemed writers, poets, and artists built their reputations there. West Bengal is also where the magnificent Bengal tiger roams the Sunderban delta near the Bay of Bengal.

Parts of the rugged coastline are draped with yellow blankets of mustard flowers, which grow in abundance in this steamy climate, along with rice and coconut palms. One local dish, a rice and lentil hodgepodge called *khichree,* is a comforting and satisfying end to any long day spent exploring West Bengal.

For a taste of the north of India try: Lamb Curry, Spicy Chicken, Plain Indian Rice, Royal Rice and Vegetables, Indian Bread, Spinach, Sesame Nut Cookies, and Sweet Rice Pudding.

THE SOUTH

The Deccan Plateau is the product of years of volcanic eruptions. Boiling lava poured across the land and then hardened to form this natural division between the north and south of India. The Western and Eastern Ghats spring up on either edge of the plateau. A long chain of hills, they are known for their dense forests and massive rocky ridges. The soil in the Ghats is arid, so farming is sparse. But as you head farther south, this trend starts to change. The tropical climate and the fertile fields of fruits, vegetables, spice plants, and coconut palms tell you that this part of India is its own unique world. As the climate changes, so do the cooking styles and ingredients. Rice replaces wheat as a staple, and coconut appears as a familiar flavoring in many dishes.

The state of Maharashtra on the Arabian Sea is a place where tradition and technology meet. Mumbai, formerly known as Bombay, is the capital and home to India's massive film and media industry often referred to as Bollywood. A city of 15 million people, Mumbai offers the best selection of restaurants in India. Large outdoor markets offer shoppers an enticing assortment of local produce, seafood, and tantalizing sweets.

Another place to sample the regional cooking of the south is Goa. Rolling hills, lush with vegetation, rice fields, palm trees, beautiful rivers, and sandy beaches are just some of the alluring sights this small state has to offer. It was in the port of Goa where for centuries so much of India's spice trade occurred. Portuguese colonists landed in the early sixteenth century and made the port not only their base but a major trading power. The culinary influence of the Portuguese is still evident today in Goan dishes, most commonly seen in the combination of peppers and vinegar.

Mountains of ground spices are sold every day in the outdoor markets of Mumbai.

The cooking of Goa features a mixture of tangy, spicy, and sweet dishes. Treasures from the Arabian Sea such as lobster, crab, and mussels find their way into the delicate recipes of the region. Local shrimp are cooked into a mild curry sweetened with coconut milk. Vinegar blends with fresh carrots and coconuts into a colorful chutney. Chutneys, sweet and tangy relishes, are common in Indian cooking. They are a perfect complement to dishes such as pork tenderloin served in a *vindaloo* sauce, another Goan specialty.

Just south of Goa is the state of Karnataka and its capital city of Bangalore. Known as the Silicon Valley of India, Bangalore is one of the nation's main technology centers. A busy, bustling city, the restaurants here are often crowded with locals and tourists alike. One of their specialties is a soup made from a snappy combination of peanuts, chiles, and ginger.

Along the southwestern tip of India is Kerala, a place of legendary natural beauty. Partially cut off from the rest of India, and long protected from invasion by the Western Ghats, Kerala is easily accessed via the waters of the Malabar Coast. Like Goa to the north, explorers once sailed great distances in search of Kerala's spices. Their complex flavors have helped make the cooking of Kerala one of India's favorite cuisines.

Avival is a prime example. Fresh garden vegetables such as carrots, tomatoes, eggplant, and peas are simmered with coconut and spices to create this delicate stew. The seafood in this coastal region is also featured in the local cuisine. Keralan cooks are known for their traditional fish and coconut stew.

The state of Tamil Nadu forms the southernmost part of India. It is found along the Coromandel and Cape Comorin by the Indian Ocean. Tamil Nadu is a combination of ancient monuments, intricate rock carvings, cooling coastal waters, and delightful mountain towns. The people of the region can trace their roots back more than 300,000 years.

The cooking there is traditionally vegetarian. Recipes are served with a cooling banana and date chutney made from locally grown produce. One dish, called *uppma,* always gets a lot of attention, as it is just as popular with children as it is with adults. Farina and vegetables are cooked with a buttery combination of spices to create this simple dish that could be called Indian "comfort food." *Uppma* is yet another example of how ancient Indian recipes are still prepared today to universal acclaim.

For a taste of the south of India try: Pork Tenderloin from Goa, Ginger and Peanut Soup, Garden Vegetable Stew, Fish and Coconut Stew, and Banana and Date Chutney.

The cooking of India is a treasure of tasty delights just waiting to be tried. So what are you waiting for? *Naush farmaiye,* or as they say in Hindi, "Please accept the joy of having a great meal."

Soups

*From top: Chicken Stock (page 18)
and Ginger and Peanut Soup (page 21)*

Chicken Stock *Yakhni*

Indian chicken stock is not only delicious, but also easy to prepare. Why not give it a try? When you make your own chicken stock, it adds a wonderful layer of flavor to any recipe that calls for it. The finished stock will keep for up to four days refrigerated or three months frozen.

Makes about 1/2 gallon

Ingredients

2 1/2 pounds chicken wings, preferably organic
1 stalk celery
1 teaspoon cumin seeds
1 teaspoon coriander seeds
2 garlic cloves
1-inch-thick slice fresh ginger
5 or 6 sprigs fresh cilantro
6 cups cold water

On your mark, get set . . .

- Rinse the chicken wings under cold water, drain, and place them in a large pot.
- Wash the celery stalk, cut it into large chunks, and add it to the pot.
- Add the cumin and coriander seeds.
- Slightly crush the garlic by laying the flat side of a large knife on the clove and pressing down firmly to break open the skin.
- Add the crushed garlic, along with the skin, to the pot.
- Lay the ginger slice on a cutting board and slightly crush it like the garlic. Add it to the pot.
- Wash the cilantro stems and leaves to remove any dirt and add them to the pot.

Cook!

- Place the pot on the stove, and then add the water. Bring to a boil over high heat.
- This will take 20 to 30 minutes.

- As the liquid comes to a boil, use a large spoon to skim off any foam or impurities that rise to the top.
- Cover the pot, leaving the lid slightly ajar. Reduce the heat to simmer and let cook for 1½ to 2 hours.
- When the stock is done, ask your adult assistant to strain it through a colander into a heat-proof bowl or pan.
- When the cooked ingredients have cooled, discard them. However, the chicken wings can be saved and are delicious as a snack.
- Any fat in the broth will rise to the top and should then be removed and discarded.
- Let the stock cool for 20 minutes. Refrigerate or freeze it.

CHEF'S TIP *Never thaw frozen stock at room temperature. Thaw it overnight in the refrigerator or in a pan on the stove over low heat.*

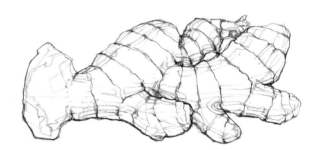

Ginger and Peanut Soup

Moongphali Shorva

The bustling, cosmopolitan city of Bangalore is home to some of India's best restaurants. This soup's delicate combination of peanuts and ginger has been a popular choice for Bangalore's diners seeking a light, yet satisfying dish. Your guests can decide just how hot they like the soup by adding their own amount of chiles. To make this soup vegetarian, substitute vegetable stock for chicken stock.

Serves 6

Ingredients

4 to 5 sprigs fresh cilantro
1 medium red onion
1 clove garlic
1-inch-thick slice fresh ginger
1 lime
1 tablespoon cornstarch blended with 1/4 cup water
2 teaspoons kosher salt
1/2 teaspoon freshly ground black pepper
4 tablespoons Usli Ghee (page 34) or extra-virgin olive oil

1/2 teaspoon turmeric
1/2 cup creamy peanut butter
4 cups Chicken Stock (page 18) or canned low-sodium vegetable broth
1/3 cup heavy cream, or milk, or a combination of both
3 green onions
1/2 cup chopped peanuts, cashews, or almonds
2 jalapeño chiles

On your mark . . .

- **Wash the cilantro to remove any dirt.**
- **Shake off the excess water and wrap it in a paper towel to dry.**
- **Finely chop the cilantro, measure 1 tablespoon, and set aside.**
- **Peel and cut the onion in half lengthwise. Lay the onion flat side down on a cutting board.**
- **Cut each half into thin slices.**
- **Measure 1 1/2 cups and set aside.**
- **Slightly crush the garlic by laying the flat side of a large knife on the clove and pressing down firmly to break open the skin.**
- **Remove and discard the skin, chop the garlic, and set aside.**
- **Using a vegetable peeler or paring knife, remove the outer skin from the ginger and discard.**

- Cut the ginger into thin slices. Stack the slices on top of each other and then cut them lengthwise into long strips. Finely chop or mince the ginger strips into tiny pieces and set aside.
- Cut the lime in half, squeeze the juice into a small bowl, and remove the seeds.
- Measure 2 tablespoons of the lime juice and set aside.
- Measure the peanut butter and set aside.
- Combine the cornstarch and water in a small bowl to form a smooth paste; this is called a slurry. Place the slurry near the stove.

Get set . . .

- Wash the green onions, cut off the root end, and remove any dark or discolored leaves.
- Finely chop the green onions, place them in a small serving bowl, and set aside.
- Chop the nuts and place them in a small serving bowl.
- Slip on a pair of kitchen gloves.
- Cut the jalapeño peppers in half lengthwise.
- Remove the seeds by running the pepper under cold water and scraping out and discarding the seeds.

- Chop the chiles into small pieces and place them in a small serving bowl.
- Rinse, dry, and remove the gloves.
- Cover each of the small serving bowls with plastic wrap and set aside.

Cook!

- Heat the ghee or oil over medium heat for 30 seconds.
- Add the cilantro, garlic, ginger, and turmeric. Mix well.
- Add the onions, mix well, and cook for 6 to 8 minutes, or until the onions are lightly browned and soft.
- Add the peanut butter, stirring well to help melt it into the other ingredients.
- Add the stock and the lime juice, and stir into a smooth liquid.
- Bring the soup to a boil. This will take about 6 to 8 minutes.
- Once the soup boils, reduce the heat and simmer for 6 to 7 minutes, stirring occasionally.
- Remix the cornstarch and water slurry. Add it to the simmering soup in a steady stream, stirring to be sure the cornstarch doesn't become lumpy.
- Add the salt and pepper and cook for 2 to 3 minutes.
- Add the milk and/or cream, blend well, and cook for another minute or until the soup is steaming hot, but not boiling.
- Serve in individual bowls.
- Pass the green onions, nuts, and chopped chiles to each guest inviting them to add them to the soup according to their own taste.
- Make sure to provide a small spoon or fork for dishing out the hot chiles.

Bread, Chutneys, Cheese, & Cooking Oil

Clockwise from left: Fresh Indian Cheese (page 32), Indian Bread (page 27), Banana and Date Chutney (page 30), Carrot Chutney (page 31), and Plain Indian Rice (page 38)

Indian Bread *Chapati*

The kitchens of India are often filled with the aroma of baking bread as it is made fresh for each meal. The baking is done on top of the stove, not in the oven. These flatbreads will take a little practice to get them just right, so be patient. Don't worry if they are not perfectly round. They are handmade, so each one will be a slightly different shape.

Makes 16

Ingredients

1 level cup whole-wheat flour
1 level cup unbleached all-purpose flour plus
  ½ cup for dusting and rolling
2 teaspoons vegetable oil, Usli Ghee (page 34),
  or melted butter

1 teaspoon kosher salt
1 cup water
3 tablespoons melted butter, optional

On your mark, get set . . .

- **Prepare your work surface for kneading the dough by sprinkling a little flour on a clean countertop or cutting board. Have a little extra flour close by to use as needed.**
- **Wash your hands.**
- **Sift the flours and salt together into a large bowl.**
- **Pour the vegetable oil, ghee, or melted butter over the flour.**
- **Now add the water all at once.**
- **Using your hands, mix the ingredients together between the palms of your hands.**

- **Repeat this step a few times until the ingredients are roughly combined and form a ball of dough.**
- **Lift the dough out of the bowl and place it onto the counter. Begin kneading by pushing the dough away from you with the palms of your hands. Fold the dough in half. Give the dough a small turn and repeat the action of pushing the dough away, folding in half, and turning it.**

- Knead the dough for 5 to 6 minutes. It will be sticky at first, but don't worry, you can add more flour as needed, but no more than a tablespoon.
- From time to time, give the dough a few punches to get the air out. Knead it until it is smooth and springy.
- Place the dough in a lightly floured bowl. Dust the top lightly with flour, cover with a clean cloth, and let the dough rest for at least 30 minutes.
- Clean the work surface where the dough was kneaded.

Cook!

- **Preheat the oven to 250°F.**
- Lightly dust the work surface and a rolling pin with flour.
- Have a small bowl of the extra 1/2 cup flour next to the work area where the dough will be kneaded.
- Knead the dough a little to warm it up.
- Cut the dough in half. Cover one half with a damp cloth while you work on the other half.
- Using your fingertips, roll the dough into a long rope.

- Cut the rope into 8 pieces.
- Shape each piece of dough into a ball and roll it in a little of the flour.
- Place the balls in a medium bowl and cover with a cloth.
- The rolling and baking of the breads requires teamwork, so it's a good idea to have your adult assistant help. One person rolls out the dough, and the other bakes it.
- Place an ovenproof serving dish with a lid in the oven.
- Take 1 ball of dough and flatten it on the work surface with the palm of your hand.
- Sprinkle a little flour on both sides of the flattened dough.
- Roll it into a 5- to 6-inch circle. The dough may stick to the work surface and the rolling pin, so dust them with a lot of the extra flour.

- Repeat this step until all the breads are rolled out.
- Cover the breads with a damp cloth.
- If you are using the melted butter, put it in a small pot over very low heat.
- In the meantime, your assistant can start baking the breads.
- Heat a nonstick frying pan or a heavy-bottomed enameled or cast-iron frying pan over low heat for about 4 to 5 minutes.
- When the pan is hot but not smoking, pick up one round of bread dough, pass it back and forth between the palms of your hands to remove any excess flour, and then place it in the frying pan.

- Bake it on one side for about 2 to 3 minutes. Use a pair of tongs to move the bread back and forth as it bakes and to turn it over.
- Bake on the other side for another 2 minutes. The bread should be lightly browned with spots on it.
- If using the melted butter, brush one side of the bread with a little of the butter.
- Place the finished breads in the ovenproof baking dish and cover with a sheet of aluminum foil and the lid to keep them warm.
- Continue with the rest of the dough until the breads are all baked. Serve warm.

CHEF'S TIP *The bread dough can be made with a food processor. Ask your adult assistant for help. Just follow the manufacturer's instructions for making bread dough, but use the quantities listed above, then simply follow the procedure for baking the breads.*

Banana and Date Chutney

Keta aur Kajur Chutney

Chutneys are similar to relishes except they combine both sweet and tangy ingredients. They have been a part of India's cuisine for centuries. This recipe is a south Indian delight and comes from the region of Tamil Nadu.

Serves 4 to 6

Ingredients

4 ripe bananas
1 medium-size red onion
1 cup chopped pitted dates
2 tablespoons candied or crystallized ginger

3/4 cup white vinegar
1 teaspoon curry powder
1/2 teaspoon coarse/kosher salt
3/4 cup molasses

On your mark, get set . .

- Peel the bananas and cut them crosswise into 1-inch slices.
- Peel and chop the onions into small chunks.
- Chop the dates if they are not already chopped. Dates are time consuming to chop, so it is best to do them in small batches. Always be on the lookout for pits, which you must remove.
- Chop the ginger into small chunks and set aside.

Cook!

- In a small saucepan, add the bananas, onions, dates, and vinegar.
- Bring to a boil, reduce the heat to medium, and cook for 12 to 15 minutes or until the onions are tender.
- Remove the pan from the heat and, using a metal spoon, mash the mixture into a smooth paste.
- Add the ginger, curry powder, salt, and molasses.
- Cook over low heat for 25 to 30 minutes until the mixture is a deep golden brown, stirring occasionally to prevent it from sticking. If the chutney sticks, lower the heat.
- Let cool completely before serving.
- This chutney will keep for up to 10 days refrigerated.

Carrot Chutney *Gajar ki Chutney*

Chutneys are an important part of any Indian meal as their sweetness complements the deep, spicy flavors of most Indian cooking. The state of Goa gives us this fresh, colorful, crunchy chutney.

Serves 4 to 6

Ingredients

1 pound carrots
½ cup light brown sugar
¾ cup white vinegar
2 green cardamom pods

¼ teaspoon freshly ground fennel seeds
½ teaspoon salt
½ cup shredded unsweetened coconut

On your mark, get set . . .

- **Wash and peel the carrots.**
- **Grate the carrots into a bowl using the largest holes of a box grater.**
- **Stop grating 1 inch from the top of the carrots.**

Cook!

- **Place all the ingredients in a medium saucepan.**
- **Bring to a boil and cook for about 4 minutes.**
- **Transfer the chutney to a bowl and allow it to cool before serving.**
- **Carrot chutney will keep for up to 1 week in the refrigerator.**

Fresh Indian Cheese *Paneer*

In this simple recipe, whole milk becomes *paneer*, a delicate cheese that is an essential ingredient in many dishes. Fresh cheeses are a staple in Indian recipes because of their clean light taste. If you have never made homemade cheese, this is the perfect recipe to try.

Makes 4 to 6

Ingredients

1 to 2 limes
1/4 cup cold water
1/2 gallon whole milk, preferably organic

On your mark, get set . . .

- Cut the lime in half, squeeze and strain the juice, measure 1/4 cup, combine with the cold water, and place the mixture next to the stove.
- Line a metal strainer with 3 to 4 layers of cheesecloth that hang a few inches over the rim of the strainer.
- Place the strainer over a large heat-proof bowl or pan.
- Cut a 12-inch piece of cotton twine and have it close by.

Cook!

- In a large 4- or 6-quart pan, bring the milk to boil over medium-high heat. This will take about 10 to 12 minutes.
- Make sure the pan is deep enough so there is room for the milk to bubble up as it boils but not spill over the sides.
- Stir the milk occasionally to keep it from sticking or burning.
- As the milk comes to a boil, the surface will become covered with tiny bubbles. Keep your eye on the milk after that happens, as it will quickly come to a full boil. When it is at full boil, lower the heat to simmer.
- Slowly pour in the lime-and-water mixture in a slow, steady stream, gently stirring the milk. Almost immediately, you will see the milk separate into curds or small chunks. The curds will separate from the whey, the pale-colored liquid in the pan.
- Stir for a few seconds and then turn off the burner and remove the pan from the heat. Let the milk stand for 5 minutes to help firm the curds.

- Ask your adult assistant to pour the entire contents of the pan through the cheesecloth-lined strainer to catch the curds. The whey can be saved, or it can be discarded.★
- Let the curds cool for about 5 minutes.
- When cool, gather the edges of the cheesecloth into a sack around the curds and give it a gentle squeeze to remove the excess liquid.
- Tie the top of the cheesecloth firmly with the string into a compact bundle. Rinse the bundle under cold water, and place the bundle into a colander in the sink with a small plate on top.
- Now find a heavy object, such as a large can of tomatoes, and set it on the plate to compress the cheese, remove the excess water, and give the finished cheese a round shape.
- Let the cheese drain and compress for 1½ hours, and then refrigerate it for at least 1 hour before using or serving.

★ *The whey, or liquid, that separates in the process of cheese making is delicious in smoothies or can replace the water when cooking vegetables. The flavor is great, and it's good for you. So why waste it?*

Indian Clarified Butter *Usli Ghee*

Many cooks today are divided over the health aspects of using ghee versus a lighter vegetable or olive oil. This recipe is presented as an option. If you are concerned about saturated fat, ghee may not be the right choice for you.

Makes 1 1/2 cups

Ingredients

1 pound unsalted butter
Cheesecloth

On your mark, get set, melt!

- Place a clean, dry metal strainer lined with 3 layers of cheesecloth over a clean, dry, heat-proof bowl.
- You will need the help of your adult assistant for this recipe. Use a 2-quart heavy-bottomed pan, preferably cast iron, or enameled cast iron.
- Melt the butter completely. This will take 6 to 8 minutes.
- Stir the butter frequently as it is melting, being very careful not to splash yourself.
- As the butter is melting, white foam will rise to the surface.

- Lower the heat to simmer, and cook for 20 to 30 minutes.
- The ghee is done when the foam on top of the butter turns brown and the crackling or popping has stopped. Carefully skim the browned foam from the top and discard.

- Turn off the stove, remove the ghee from the heat, and cool for 10 to 15 minutes.
- Carefully pour the cool ghee into the cheesecloth-lined strainer.

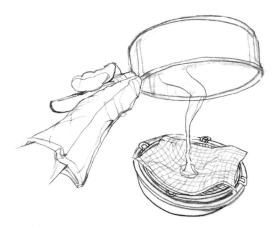

- The ghee should be golden in color, with no residue on it.
- If you find after straining it that it still has residue or milk particles in it, strain it one more time through the cheesecloth.
- Pour the finished ghee into a clean glass jar. Let cool completely, cover, and refrigerate.
- The ghee will keep for 1 month refrigerated.

Rice
Dishes
&
Spice

Royal Rice and Vegetables (page 39)

Plain Indian Rice *Chaval*

Rice is an essential part of every Indian meal. The most famous rice in India is basmati, which means the "fragrant one" in Hindi. It grows along the snow-fed rivers threading out of the Himalayas. This silky, delicate, long-grain rice with its nutty fragrance and unforgettable flavor is regarded as the king of rice. That's saying a lot considering there are thousands of varieties of rice to choose from. You can find basmati rice in supermarkets or Indian specialty stores. Any long-grain rice will work for the recipes in this book, just prepare according to instructions on the package. Why not try basmati for an authentic taste of India?

Serves 4

Ingredients

1 cup basmati rice
1¾ cups cold water
½ teaspoon kosher salt, optional

On your mark, get set . . .

- **Place the rice in a bowl.**
- **Fill the bowl with cold water and, using your very clean hands, swirl the rice around to help remove the starch.**
- **Carefully pour off the water, but not the rice.**
- **Repeat this step 7 to 8 times, or until the water is clear.**
- **After the final rinse, cover the rice with the 1¾ cup of cold water and set aside to soak for 20 to 30 minutes.**

Cook!

- **Bring the water, rice, and salt to a boil over high heat in a 2-quart pan, stirring occasionally.**
- **Lower the heat to simmer, partially cover the pan, and cook for 10 minutes.**
- **Place the lid firmly on the pan and cook for 5 minutes more.**
- **Remove the pan from the heat and let the rice rest 5 additional minutes. Fluff with a fork and serve hot.**

Royal Rice and Vegetables *Ratan Pulao*

This dish is a pleasure to behold, with its raisins, spices, and colorful vegetables mixed in with the white rice—and it looks as good as it tastes. It can be served as a vegetarian entrée or as a delicious addition to serve alongside lamb or chicken curry. When shopping for the ingredients for this recipe, look for the freshest vegetables, preferably organic. If you don't have any luck finding fresh vegetables, you can always use frozen ones. Just remember to select a good quality and partially thaw them first.

Serves 4 to 6

Ingredients

1 2/3 cups basmati or long-grain rice
2 medium-size carrots, or 6 ounces frozen
6 ounces (1 1/4 cups) fresh or frozen green peas
2 ounces green beans (1/2 cup), fresh or frozen
2 ears fresh corn or 4 ounces (1 cup) frozen
1 jalapeño or serrano chile
1/4 cup vegetable oil or ghee
1 teaspoon cumin seeds
1 1/2-inch piece cinnamon stick

4 whole cloves
4 whole green cardamom pods
8 black peppercorns
1 1/2 teaspoons kosher salt
2 1/2 cups of hot water
1 small red bell pepper
1/4 cup raisins
1/4 cup sliced almonds

On your mark . . .

- **Place the rice in a large bowl.**
- **Fill the bowl with cold water and, using your very clean hands, swirl the rice around to help remove the starch. Carefully pour off the water.**
- **Repeat this step 7 to 8 times or until the water is clear.**
- **After the final rinse, cover the rice with 2 inches of cold water, and set the bowl aside to soak.**

Get set . . .

- **Cut the tops off the carrots, then wash and peel them.**
- **Cut the carrots in half lengthwise.**
- **Lay the carrots flat side down and cut each half lengthwise into 1/2-inch-wide strips.**
- **Stack the strips on top of each other and cut them into 1/2-inch cubes. Place in a bowl and set aside.**
- **If using frozen carrots, thaw them partially and add to the bowl.**

- If using fresh peas, remove them from the shell. To do this, take a pea pod and gently press on the seam to separate the halves. Gently pry the pod open until you see the peas inside. Carefully remove the peas to a bowl and discard the pod. Repeat until you have shelled all the peas, then set them aside.

- Measure 1ɪ/4 cups peas, fresh or frozen, and add them to the bowl with the carrots.
- Wash the green beans in cold water and remove the stem from the top.
- Cut off any discolored tips from the bottom and discard.
- If using frozen beans, let them defrost in a bowl.
- Cut the cleaned or defrosted beans into ɪ/2-inch slices and add them to the bowl with the carrots and peas.
- If using fresh corn, remove the husks and the silk from the cob.
- Ask your adult assistant to help with this next step. Stand the corn upright. Using a sharp knife, slice the kernels off the cob. Keep turning the cob until the kernels are removed. Scoop up the kernels, measure 1 cup, and add to the bowl of vegetables.

- If using frozen corn, partially thaw the corn, measure 1 cup, and add to the bowl of vegetables.
- You will need a total of 3 cups of the combined vegetables.
- Drain the rice in a colander.
- Slip on a pair of kitchen gloves.

- Cut the chile in half and remove the stem.
- To remove the seeds, rinse the chile under cold water and scrape out and discard the seeds.
- Chop the chile into small pieces and set aside.
- Rinse, dry, and remove the gloves.

Cook!

- Heat the oil in a large 10- to 12-inch heavy-bottomed metal frying pan over medium-low heat for 1 minute.
- Add the cumin seeds. Be prepared with the lid and cover the pan when they begin to pop.
- Count to 10 and then add the cinnamon stick, cloves, whole cardamom, and peppercorns.
- Stir the spice mixture, and add the chile. Cook for 1 minute then add the vegetables. Stir well to combine everything and cook for 2 to 3 minutes, stirring frequently. Increase the heat to medium and add the drained rice.
- Cook for 3 to 4 minutes or until the rice just begins to change color.
- Add the salt and mix well.
- Now add the hot water to the rice and vegetables. Stir to combine the ingredients.
- Bring the rice to a boil, cover, reduce the heat to simmer, and cook for 15 minutes.
- In the meantime, wash the bell pepper and remove the stem from the top.
- Slice the bell pepper in half and remove the seeds.
- Cut the halves lengthwise into 1/4-inch-wide strips.
- Cut the strips crosswise into 1/2-inch pieces, measure 1/2 cup, and set aside.
- After 15 minutes, remove the pan from the heat and let it rest for 5 minutes. Don't open the lid.
- When ready to serve, remove the lid and gently mix in the raisins, bell pepper, and almonds with a fork. Remove the cinnamon stick.
- Serve hot, mounded on a platter.

CHEF'S TIP *Inform your guests that the whole spices in the dish are perfectly safe to eat, but eating them is not recommended.*

Garam Masala *Indian Spice Mixture*

Masala means "mixture" in Hindi. Countless recipes in Indian cooking use a masala to achieve the unique flavor of the dish. Here is a blend of spices that you can prepare in your kitchen and use for several of the recipes in this book. Garam masala is also available in many supermarkets and specialty stores. But once you discover how much better the flavor is when it is freshly roasted and ground, you will do what the Indian cook does and prepare your garam masala at home.

Makes 1/2 cup

Ingredients

1 tablespoon black peppercorns
2- to 3-inch-long piece cinnamon stick
2 tablespoons whole cloves
4 tablespoons black cardamom pods
4 tablespoons cumin seeds
1 teaspoon freshly grated nutmeg

On your mark, get set . . .

- **Preheat the oven to 200°F for 10 minutes.**
- **Place all the spices, except the nutmeg, on a baking sheet.**

Cook!

- **Place the baking sheet in the preheated oven and roast the spices for 20 to 30 minutes.**
- **Every so often, open the oven and give the baking sheet a gentle shake to move the spices around and to prevent them from burning.**
- **Remove and let the spices cool a little on the baking sheet.**
- **Remove the outer pods from the cardamom.**
- **To do this, place the pods on a clean kitchen towel. Fold the towel in half over the pods and, using a rolling pin, gently crush the pods to open. You just want to break open the pods, so be careful not to flatten them too much or you will destroy the seeds inside. Remove the shells and pick out the seeds inside.**
- **Grind the spices in a clean spice or coffee grinder and place in a clean glass jar. Garam masala will keep fresh up to 4 months.**

Vegetable Dishes

From left: Fresh Indian Cheese with Peas, Tomatoes, and Mint (page 52), Garden Vegetable Stew with Coconut (page 47), and Spinach (page 50)

Garden Vegetable Stew with Coconut *Avival*

Rich in history and natural beauty, Kerala is a jewel on the shore of the Arabian Sea. *Avival* is one of the specialties of this breathtaking region. Fresh vegetables, flavorful spices, and coconut are common ingredients in the dishes made along India's Spice Coast. Look for vegetables that are in season in your area when shopping for this recipe.

Serves 4 to 6

Ingredients

1 small plum tomato
1 small green onion
1/4 teaspoon freshly ground cumin
1/8 teaspoon cayenne pepper
1/8 teaspoon turmeric
1 cup shredded unsweetened coconut
1/2 cup water plus 2 tablespoons if needed
1 medium-size Yukon gold potato
2 medium-size carrots

1/4 pound (1 cup) green beans
1 small red bell pepper
1 cup (4 ounces) peas, fresh or frozen
1 small Japanese eggplant
1 to 2 jalapeño or serrano peppers, or to taste
1 1/2 teaspoon salt
1/4 teaspoon turmeric
1/4 teaspoon cayenne pepper
1 cup cold water

On your mark . . .

- Wash the tomato and cut out the stem circle from the top.
- Cut the tomato into chunks, measure 1 cup, and place them into the blender.
- Wash the green onion, cut off the root end, and remove any dark or discolored parts. Cut into 1/4-inch slices, and add to the blender.
- Add the ground cumin, cayenne pepper, turmeric, shredded coconut, and water to the blender.
- Press the lid firmly into place and blend at high speed for 30 seconds, or until you have a smooth paste.
- Open the lid and scrape down the sides of the blender. Add a few more tablespoons of water if needed to allow the paste to blend.
- Remove the paste with a rubber spatula to a small bowl and set aside.

Get set . . .

- Wash the potato but don't peel it.
- Cut the potato in half.

- Lay the flat side face down on the cutting board and cut it into 1-inch-thick slices.
- Stack the slices on top of each other and cut them lengthwise into thin matchsticks or strips about 1/2 inch wide.

- Cut the matchsticks crosswise into sections 2 inches long.
- Repeat with the rest of the potato, measure 1 cup, place in a large bowl of cold water, and set aside.
- Cut the tops off the carrots, then wash and peel them.
- Repeat the same procedure as the potatoes, and cut the carrots into matchsticks the same size as the potatoes. Measure 1 cup and add to the potatoes.
- Wash and trim the green beans removing the stem at the top.
- Cut off any discolored tips from the bottom and discard.
- Cut the beans into 1 1/2-inch-long sections, and add to the bowl.
- Wash the bell pepper and cut out the stem at the top.
- Cut the bell pepper in half, remove the seeds from the inside, and then cut the halves into strips 1/2 inch wide and 1 1/2 inches long. Add the bell pepper to the bowl.
- Wash the eggplant, cut into 1-inch-thick slices, and add to the bowl.
- If using fresh peas, remove the shells. To do this take one pea pod and gently press on the seam to separate the halves of the pod. Gently pry the pod open until you see the peas inside. Carefully remove the peas to a bowl and discard the pod. Repeat until you have shelled all the peas. Measure 1 cup, and add to the other vegetables.
- If using frozen peas, measure 1 cup (they don't have to be thawed), and place them in a separate bowl to be added later.
- Slip on a pair of kitchen gloves.
- Cut the hot peppers in half and remove the stem.

- To remove the seeds, rinse the pepper under cold water and then scrape out and discard them.
- Slice the peppers in half lengthwise, cut them into strips, chop them into small pieces, and add to the vegetables.
- Rinse, dry, and remove the gloves.
- You should have a total of 3 1/2 to 4 cups vegetables.

Cook!

- Place all the vegetables, except the frozen peas, into a large pot.
- Add the salt, turmeric, cayenne pepper, and water. Toss gently with a spoon, not your hands, to combine and evenly coat all the ingredients.
- Bring the pot to a boil over high heat.
- Once it boils, set the lid slightly ajar, lower the heat to medium-low, and boil for 5 minutes.
- After 5 minutes, add the frozen peas, if you are using them.
- Add the coconut paste and gently toss all the ingredients together with a spoon.

- Reduce the heat to simmer, place the lid slightly ajar on the pot, and simmer the vegetables for 10 minutes or until tender and cooked through.
- If the sauce is too thick to simmer as they cook, add more water, but not more than 1/4 cup.
- Spoon the finished stew onto a serving platter and serve hot.
- This recipe may be made ahead of time and reheated when ready to serve.

Spinach *Saag*

If you are not a fan of this leafy green, then perhaps a sweet, buttery sauce made with crunchy cashews and currants will change your mind about eating your spinach. There are many versions of this dish in Indian cooking. This one comes from Punjab in the north of India.

Serves 6

Ingredients

The Spinach

2 pounds fresh or frozen spinach
2 jalapeño peppers
1 1/2-inch-thick slice fresh ginger
1/3 cup currants
1/2 cup raw cashews

1 tablespoon kosher salt
4 tablespoons ghee or melted butter
1 teaspoon sugar
1/2 teaspoon Garam Masala (page 43)

The Spice Mix

2 whole cloves
1/4 teaspoon fennel seeds
1/4 teaspoon yellow mustard seeds
1/4 teaspoon cumin seeds

On your mark . . .

If using fresh spinach:
- **Cut the stems off the spinach and discard.**
- **Fill a clean sink with cold water.**
- **Separate the leaves and drop them into the water.**
- **Let them soak for a few minutes, gently moving them around with your hands to help remove any dirt.**
- **Carefully lift the spinach into a colander, being careful not to disturb the water too much.**
- **Drain the water from the sink and clean any dirt or sand from the bottom.**
- **Refill the sink with cold water and repeat the washing at least once.**
- **If there is still sand or dirt in the sink, repeat a final time.**
- **Drain the spinach in a colander.**

If using frozen spinach:

- Thaw the spinach completely in a bowl and set aside.

Get set . . .

- Put the currants into a small bowl, cover them with 1/2 cup of warm water, and set aside.
- Slip on a pair of kitchen gloves and slice the jalapeño in half lengthwise.
- Remove the seeds by running the pepper under water and scraping them out.
- Finely chop or mince the peppers and set aside.
- Rinse, dry, and remove the gloves.
- Peel the outer skin from the ginger with a vegetable peeler or paring knife and discard.
- Cut the ginger into thin slices. Stack the slices on top of each other and then cut them into long strips. Finely chop or mince the ginger strips into tiny pieces and set aside.
- Place all the ingredients for the spice mix into a clean spice or coffee grinder.
- Grind for about 20 seconds into a coarse powder.
- Place the ground spices in a small bowl and set aside.
- Unplug the grinder, wipe it, then wash and dry the lid.
- Chop the cashews into chunks and set aside.

Cook!

- Bring a large 6- to 8-quart pot of water to a boil.
- When the water boils, add 1 tablespoon salt and then the spinach. Cook for 4 to 5 minutes.
- Ask your adult assistant to drain the spinach in a colander.
- Using the back of a spoon, gently press on the spinach to remove the excess water.
- Drain the currants and pat them dry on a paper towel.
- Melt the ghee or butter in a 10- to 12-inch frying pan over medium heat.
- Add the chopped peppers, ginger, and the spice mix. Cook for 1 minute.
- Add the cashews, sugar, and currants. Cook for 3 to 4 minutes or until the nuts just begin to turn brown.
- Place the drained spinach on a serving plate.
- Pour the nuts, currants, and spice mixture over the spinach.
- Sprinkle on the garam masala and serve hot.

Fresh Indian Cheese with Peas, Tomatoes, and Mint *Matar Paneer*

This vegetarian recipe comes from the Punjab region in the north. This dish uses *paneer*, or homemade Fresh Indian Cheese (page 32). If you don't have the time to make your own cheese, you can substitute tofu. This recipe works best if you make it ahead of time and let its subtle flavor develop as the cheese absorbs the blend of spices. It can, however, be served as soon as it's ready. This recipe calls for a blender, so ask your adult assistant to help with these steps.

Serves 4

Ingredients

1 10-ounce package frozen baby peas
   (1 cup), or 1 1/2 pounds fresh peas
2 pounds fresh tomatoes, or 1 28-ounce
   can chopped tomatoes
5 to 6 sprigs fresh mint or 1 tablespoon dried
5 to 6 sprigs fresh cilantro
1 to 2 jalapeño peppers
1-inch-thick piece fresh ginger
1/4 cup water
2 teaspoons freshly ground coriander
1/2 teaspoon paprika

1 teaspoon turmeric
1 1/2 cups Fresh Indian Cheese (page 32),
   or 1 1/2 cups extra-firm tofu
1 teaspoon cumin seeds
1/2 teaspoon black or yellow mustard seeds
1/4 teaspoon fennel seeds
1 teaspoon salt
1 teaspoon granulated sugar
2 teaspoons Garam Masala (page 43)
1/2 cup vegetable oil, melted butter, or ghee

On your mark . . .

- **If using frozen peas, remove them from the package and place in a strainer, rinse under cold running water, and set aside to drain.**
- **If using fresh peas, remove them from their shells. Take one pea pod and gently press on the seam to separate the halves of the pod. Gently pry the pod open until you see the peas inside. Carefully remove the peas to a bowl and discard the pod.**
- **Repeat until you have shelled all the peas, measure 1 cup, and add to the other vegetables.**
- **If using fresh tomatoes, remove the stem circle from the top and discard.**
- **Chop the tomatoes into small chunks, measure 2 cups, and set aside.**
- **If using canned tomatoes, measure 2 cups with the liquid and set aside.**

- Wash the fresh mint and cilantro.
- Shake off the excess water and wrap in a paper towel to dry them.
- Chop the two herbs together, measure 3 tablespoons, place in a small bowl, cover, and set aside.

Get set . . .

- Slip on a pair of kitchen gloves.
- Cut the peppers in half lengthwise and remove the stem.
- To remove the seeds, rinse the pepper under cold water, then scrape out and discard the seeds.
- Chop the peppers into chunks and place them in a blender.
- Rinse, dry, and remove the gloves.
- Using a vegetable peeler or sharp paring knife, peel the outer skin from the ginger and discard.
- Cut the ginger into 1/4-inch slices. Stack the slices on top of each other and then cut them into long strips.
- Add the strips of ginger to the blender.
- Add the water, ground coriander, paprika, and turmeric and press the lid firmly into place.
- Blend at high speed for 30 to 40 seconds until combined into a paste.
- Pour the paste into a small bowl and place the bowl near the stove.
- Cut the cheese or tofu into 1/2-inch-thick slices, then cut the slices into 1/2-inch cubes. Place in a separate bowl and set aside.

Cook!

- Add 4 tablespoons of the vegetable oil, ghee, or melted butter to a 4- to 6-quart heavy-bottomed saucepan.
- Heat the oil over medium heat for 30 to 40 seconds. Add about one-third of the cheese or tofu cubes and lightly fry them until they just start to turn brown.
- Use a slotted, metal spoon to gently move them back and forth in the pan and brown them evenly. Be careful not to break the cubes.

- Remove the cubes to a bowl and repeat this step until all the cheese or tofu cubes are browned.
- Add the cumin, mustard, and fennel seeds to the pan and cook for about 1 minute.
- Be prepared to cover the pan for a few seconds as the spices cook; they are likely to pop and spatter.
- Once the popping stops, remove the lid and add 4 more tablespoons of the oil, ghee, or melted butter.
- Add the spice paste to the frying pan and stir well to combine. Fry the paste for about 2 to 3 minutes, then add the chopped tomatoes.
- Cook for 8 to 10 minutes or until the liquid has reduced by one-half.
- Add the peas and bring back to a boil.
- Add the salt and sugar, cover, and reduce the heat to low.
- If using fresh peas, cook for 15 minutes.
- If using frozen peas, cook for 5 to 7 minutes.

- Add the cheese or tofu cubes, gently stir to combine, and heat through for about 5 minutes.
- Remove from the heat, cover the pan, and let it stand for 30 minutes to 1 hour.
- When ready to serve, reheat on low for 5 minutes, or until warmed through.
- Sprinkle on the garam masala, the chopped mint and cilantro, and serve warm.

Main Dishes

From left: Spicy Chicken (page 62) and
Pork Tenderloin from Goa (page 64)

Lamb Curry *Shahi Gosht*

This dish originated in the elegant courts of the Moghul empire and comes from the Kashmir Valley. It is a great way to show off your Indian cooking skills. When shopping for the ingredients, look for lamb cubes that are used for kebabs, or ask the butcher at your market to cut the lamb into cubes for you. If you can't find cubed lamb, beef will work just as well. Simply adjust the cooking time as indicated in the recipe. This recipe also calls for a blender, so ask your adult assistant to help with those steps. Once you bring this dish to the table, you might be called *shahi,* which means "royal." Just don't let it go to your head.

Serves 6

Ingredients

The Spice Mix

1 teaspoon turmeric
2 teaspoons freshly ground coriander
1/2 teaspoon ground mace
1 teaspoon freshly ground cinnamon
1 teaspoon fennel seeds
2 teaspoons salt

The Lamb Stew

2 pounds lean lamb or beef stew sirloin cut into 1 1/2-inch cubes
2 medium-size yellow onions
6 to 8 sprigs fresh cilantro or mint
1 jalapeño chile
1 1/2-inch-thick piece fresh ginger
2 garlic cloves
1 teaspoon cumin seeds

1 teaspoon black or yellow mustard seeds
1/2 teaspoon cayenne pepper, optional
1/4 cup cold water
1/4 cup vegetable oil or ghee
1 cup unflavored whole-milk yogurt
1/2 cup sour cream

On your mark . . .

- **Combine the salt with the ingredients in the spice mix in a small bowl.**
- **Place the lamb or beef cubes in a large bowl.**
- **Pour the spice mix over the meat. Using a large spoon, toss the meat cubes and spices together until evenly coated. Don't use your hands to combine the meat and spices; turmeric will stain your hands.**

- Allow the meat and spices to marinate for 15 to 30 minutes at room temperature. If you think it will take you longer to continue the recipe, refrigerate the meat until ready to proceed.

Get set . . .

- Peel the onions and cut in half across the middle. Slice each onion half into thin rings.
- Measure 2 1/2 cups onion rings and set aside.
- Wash the cilantro or mint to remove any dirt. Shake off the excess water, wrap in a paper towel, and set aside.
- Slip on a pair of kitchen gloves.
- Cut the chile in half and remove the stem.
- To remove the seeds, rinse the chile under cold water then scrape out and discard the seeds.
- Chop the chile into small pieces, measure 1 tablespoon, and set aside.

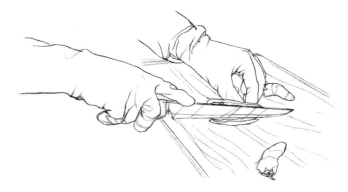

- Rinse, dry, and remove the gloves.
- Peel the outer skin from the ginger with a vegetable peeler or paring knife and discard.
- Cut the ginger crosswise into thin slices.
- Stack the slices on top of each other and then cut them into long strips. Chop the ginger strips into pieces and set aside.
- Slightly crush the garlic by laying the flat side of a chef's knife on the clove and pressing evenly to break open the skin.
- Remove and discard the skin, chop the garlic into small chunks, and set aside.
- In a blender, add the garlic, ginger, cumin seeds, mustard seeds, cayenne pepper, and the water.

- Press the lid firmly into place and blend at high speed for 30 to 40 seconds or until smooth. This is the spice paste.
- Add more water if needed, but not more than 2 tablespoons.
- Remove the spice paste to a small bowl and place near the stove.
- Chop the cilantro or mint and set aside.

Cook!

- Add the oil to a 10- to 12-inch heavy-bottomed frying pan.
- Heat the oil over medium heat for 30 to 40 seconds.
- Add the onions and fry for 8 to 10 minutes, or until golden brown.
- Stir frequently to prevent sticking or burning.
- Add the chopped chile and cook for 2 minutes.
- Add the spice paste and cook for 3 to 5 minutes, stirring to prevent sticking and lowering the heat if necessary.
- Add the meat cubes, return the heat to medium, and cook for 5 to 6 minutes, stirring frequently until the meat begins to brown.
- When the meat is browned, pour off and discard any excess fat in the pan.
- In the meantime, combine the yogurt and sour cream and pour it over the meat.
- Stir well to combine all the ingredients as you bring the pan to a gentle boil; the temperature should not be too high, or the yogurt and sour cream will separate.
- Reduce the heat to simmer, cover the pan with the lid, and cook for 45 to 50 minutes, or until the lamb is cooked through and tender. If using beef, cook an additional 10 minutes.
- Skim any fat from the surface.
- Serve hot with the fresh herbs sprinkled on top.
- Serve with Plain Indian Rice (page 38).

Spicy Chicken *Bhooni Murgh*

Allspice grows abundantly in the northern state of Kashmir. It is a strong spice with the combined aromas of cinnamon, cloves, black pepper, and nutmeg all in one small berry. The chicken in this recipe can be grilled on a barbecue with the help of your adult assistant, of course, but it works just as well baked in the oven. Either way, cooked indoors or out, it will delight you and your guests with how good it tastes.

Serves 4

Ingredients

The Spice Mix

1 teaspoon ground allspice
1/2 teaspoon cayenne pepper
1 teaspoon turmeric
1/2 teaspoon Garam Masala (page 43)
1 teaspoon ground ginger
1 1/2 teaspoons salt

The Chicken

1 3 1/2-pound skinless chicken cut into 8 to 10 pieces, or 5 skinless chicken drumsticks and 5 thighs, preferably organic

1 garlic clove
1 lime
4 tablespoons vegetable oil or ghee

On your mark, get set . . .

- **Wash the chicken pieces and dry thoroughly with paper towels.**
- **Place the chicken in a bowl large enough to hold all the pieces.**
- **Combine the ingredients for the spice mix in a small bowl.**
- **Add the spice mix to the chicken and, using a spoon, toss well to evenly coat the pieces.**
- **Slightly crush the garlic by laying the flat side of a chef's knife on the clove and pressing evenly to break open the skin.**
- **Remove and discard the skin, chop the garlic, measure 1 teaspoon, and add to the chicken.**
- **Cut the lime in half, squeeze the juice into a small bowl, remove any seeds, measure 2 teaspoons, and add to the chicken.**
- **Toss the chicken pieces a second time with the spoon and marinate for 15 to 30 minutes in the refrigerator.**

- Lightly oil an ovenproof baking dish large enough to hold all the chicken pieces and set aside.

Cook!

- **Preheat the oven to 450°F.**
- Remove the chicken from the refrigerator.
- Using a pair of tongs, place the chicken pieces in a single layer in the prepared baking dish.
- Drizzle the oil over the chicken and roll the pieces back and forth so they are evenly coated.
- Place the chicken in the preheated oven and bake for 15 minutes. Set a timer so you don't forget.
- After 15 minutes, **reduce the heat to 375°F** and continue to bake for 35 to 40 minutes.
- Serve hot or cold.

Pork Tenderloin from Goa

Vindaloo

Goa's culinary gift to the world is vindaloo. For those who think that all vindaloos are incredibly hot, this recipe might be a surprise. It has a deep, sweet, and spicy flavor that is hard to resist.

Serves 4 to 6

Ingredients

1 small onion
2 green onions
1 clove garlic
1/2 to 1 teaspoon ground cayenne pepper, to taste
3/4 teaspoon ground cinnamon
1/4 teaspoon freshly ground anise
1/2 teaspoon freshly ground cloves
1 tablespoon maple syrup
2 jalapeño chiles
1 tablespoon coarse ground mustard

1 tablespoon tomato paste
1 1/2 cups hot water or Chicken Stock, either homemade (page 18) or canned low-sodium broth
1 teaspoon salt
1/4 teaspoon freshly ground black pepper
3 tablespoons vegetable oil
2 pounds pork tenderloin (2 1-pound pieces)

On your mark, get set . . .

- **Peel and chop the onion into small chunks, measure 1 cup, and set aside.**
- **Wash the green onions, then remove the root end and any dark or discolored outer leaves.**
- **Chop the white end of the green onion and a few inches of the green tops into 1/2-inch slices and add to the onions.**
- **Slightly crush the garlic by laying the flat side of a chef's knife on the clove and pressing evenly to break open the skin. Remove and discard the skin, chop the garlic, measure 1 teaspoon, and set aside.**
- **Combine the cinnamon, anise, and cloves in a small bowl and set aside.**
- **Combine the maple syrup, mustard, tomato paste, and hot water in a small bowl.**
- **Stir well to combine all the ingredients and set aside.**
- **Slip on a pair of kitchen gloves.**
- **Cut the jalapeño chiles in half and remove the stems.**

- To remove the seeds, rinse the chile under cold water and scrape out and discard the seeds.
- Chop the chile into small pieces and set aside.
- Rinse, dry, and remove the gloves.

Cook!

- Sprinkle the tenderloins with the salt and black pepper on all sides.
- In a 10-inch metal or nonstick frying pan, heat 1 tablespoon of the oil over medium heat for 30 seconds.
- Brown the pork tenderloins on all sides. This will take about 8 minutes.
- Remove the tenderloins to a warm plate and set aside.
- Add the other 2 tablespoons of oil to the frying pan and heat for 30 seconds.
- Add the chopped jalapeño chiles and sauté for 1 minute.
- Add the onions and cook for 6 to 8 minutes, or until they turn a light golden brown.
- Add the spices, cayenne pepper, and garlic and cook for 1 minute.
- Add the tomato paste mixture and the salt. Bring to a boil.
- Add the pork tenderloins and spoon the sauce over to cover.

- Return the sauce to a boil, cover, and reduce the heat to a simmer. Cook for 35 to 40 minutes or until the pork is cooked through and tender.
- Cut the tenderloin into 1-inch slices and serve hot with the extra sauce poured over the pork.
- Serve with Plain Indian Rice (page 38).

Fish and Coconut Stew

Kerala Meen Molee

Coconuts grow in abundance in Kerala along the Spice Coast of southern India. For centuries spice merchants traveled there in search of exotic spices. One of the things they discovered in their travels was the outstanding cooking of the region. *Meen molee* is a favorite in the coastal towns along the Arabian Sea. It can be prepared with any of the different types of fish listed at the end of the recipe. Just choose the one that is the freshest. This recipe calls for a blender, so ask your adult assistant to help.

Serves 4

Ingredients

The Spice Mix

1 teaspoon freshly ground coriander
1/4 teaspoon freshly ground cumin
1/4 teaspoon turmeric
1/4 freshly ground black pepper
1 teaspoon curry powder
1 teaspoon salt

The Fish Stew

2 pounds fresh salmon fillets★
5 to 6 sprigs fresh cilantro
1 medium-size yellow onion
2-inch piece fresh ginger
2 cloves garlic
1 jalapeño or serrano chile
2 tomatoes or 1 cup canned chopped tomatoes with their liquid

1/3 cup cold water
1/2 cup unsweetened coconut milk
1/2 cup cold water
4 tablespoons vegetable oil or ghee
2 teaspoons black or yellow mustard seeds

On your mark . . .

- **Combine the ingredients for the spice mix, blend well, place in a small bowl, and set next to the stove.**
- **Rinse the fish fillets and pat dry.**
- **Place the fillets, one at a time, over an inverted bowl. Check for any small bones by running your fingers over the tops of the fillets.**

- Remove the bones by using a clean sheet of paper towel to grip the tip of the bone sticking out and pull. You can also use a clean pair of needle-nose pliers to pull out the bones.
- Cut the fish into 2-inch squares.
- Place in a bowl and refrigerate.
- Wash the cilantro to remove any dirt. Shake off the excess water and wrap in a paper towel to dry.

Get set . . .

- Peel the onions and cut them in half lengthwise.
- Place the onions flat side down on a cutting board and cut each half into thin slices, measure 2 cups, and set aside.
- Peel the outer skin from the ginger with a vegetable peeler or paring knife and discard. Cut the ginger into thin slices and add to a small bowl.
- Slightly crush the garlic by laying the flat side of a chef's knife on the clove and pressing evenly to break open the skin.
- Remove and discard the skin, cut the garlic into thin slices, and add to the ginger.
- Slip on a pair of kitchen gloves.
- Cut the chile in half lengthwise and remove the stem.
- To remove the seeds, rinse the chile under cold water and scrape out and discard the seeds. Chop the chile into small pieces, measure 2 teaspoons, and add to the bowl with the ginger and garlic.
- Rinse, dry, and remove the gloves.
- Remove the stem circle from the top of the tomato. Cut the tomato into small chunks, scoop up the tomato and any liquid, measure 1 cup, and add to the ginger and garlic.
- If using canned chopped tomatoes, measure 1 cup and some of their liquid, and add to the ginger mixture.
- Place the ginger mixture into a blender.
- Add 1/3 cup cold water.
- Press the lid firmly into place and blend at high speed for 30 seconds or until smooth. Pour the tomato-and-ginger paste into a bowl and place near the stove.
- Combine the coconut milk and water and place near the stove.

Cook!

- Heat the oil in a 12-inch heavy-bottomed metal or nonstick frying pan over medium heat for 30 to 40 seconds.
- Add the mustard seeds and cook for about 1 minute.
- Add the onions and cook for 8 to 10 minutes, or until they begin to turn golden brown.
- Stir frequently to prevent the onions from sticking.
- Add the spice mix and cook for 1 minute or until the onions have changed color.
- Now pour in the tomato-and-ginger paste, reduce the heat to low, and cook another 10 minutes. Stir frequently as the sauce thickens and reduces.
- Remove the fish pieces from the refrigerator.
- Add the coconut milk to the frying pan and stir well to combine.
- Add the fish pieces a few at a time to the frying pan.
- Once all the fish has been added, spoon some of the sauce over each piece of fish.
- Reduce the heat to low, bring the pan to a simmer, and cook uncovered for 12 to 15 minutes or until the fish is cooked through.
- Chop the fresh cilantro.
- Skim the fat from the surface.
- Serve the fish on a deep platter, pour over the sauce, and garnish with chopped cilantro.
- Serve alone or with Plain Indian Rice (page 38).

★ *You can also use red snapper, cod, sea bass, or halibut. When shopping for this recipe, it is best to look for fish fillets that are at least 3/4 inch thick rather than thinner ones.*

Desserts

From left: Sweet Rice Pudding (page 73)
and Sesame Nut Cookies (page 72)

Sesame Nut Cookies *Til Ladoos*

These cookies are similar to those sold on the streets of Jaipur in the state of Rajasthan. Each March there is a festival of elephants, and *ladoos* are the featured treats.

Makes 24 cookies

Ingredients

1 cup sesame seeds
1/2 cup chopped nuts (walnuts, almonds, or peanuts)
1/3 cup water

1/4 teaspoon ground ginger
1/4 teaspoon freshly ground cardamom
3/4 cup dark brown sugar

On your mark, get set, cook!

- **Preheat the oven to 375°F.**
- Toast the sesame seeds by placing them in a dry frying pan over low running heat and giving the pan a gentle shake every few minutes. If they start to pop, reduce the heat. Toast for 4 to 5 minutes.
- Place them in a bowl and set aside.
- Place the chopped nuts in a blender. Press the lid firmly into place and turn it on and off a few times to grind the nuts into a powder.
- Remove the nuts with a rubber spatula and add to the sesame seeds.
- Bring the water to boil in a 1-quart saucepan over high heat.
- Add the ground ginger and cardamom. Stir well to dissolve and then add the brown sugar. Stir until melted. Immediately lower the heat to simmer, and cook the sugar and water for 3 minutes.
- Pour the sugar mixture over the sesame and nuts, and stir well to combine all the ingredients into a smooth batter. Set aside to cool for about 5 minutes.
- Generously butter 2 cookie sheets.
- Using 2 teaspoons, one to scoop the batter, and one to help it slide off onto the baking sheet, drop the batter onto the cookie sheet, leaving at least 2 inches between each cookie.
- After all the batter has been placed on the sheets, use your wet fingers to shape the cookies into rounds, gently flattening them into 1 1/2-inch by 1/4-inch-thick circles.
- Bake at 375°F for 10 minutes.
- Cool the cookies on the sheet for 5 minutes, then lift them off with a spatula and transfer to a rack.

Sweet Rice Pudding *Kheer*

This popular and legendary dessert holds a place of distinction in Indian cooking. *Kheer* is served all over India, often with great fanfare, on special occasions and holidays.

Serves 6 to 8

Ingredients

1 cup basmati rice
8 to 10 whole green cardamom pods or
   1 teaspoon freshly ground cardamom
5 cups whole milk

¾ cup granulated sugar
2 tablespoons shelled, unsalted pistachios
3 tablespoons dark raisins
¼ cup sliced, blanched almonds

On your mark, get set . . .

- **Place the rice in a medium-size bowl. Fill the bowl with cold water and swirl the rice around to help remove the starch.**
- **Carefully pour off the water, making sure not to pour out the rice that has settled to the bottom. Repeat this step 7 to 8 times, or until the water is clear.**
- **Fill the bowl one last time with enough cold water to cover the rice by 2 inches. Let the rice soak for 30 minutes.**
- **Pour the rice in a strainer and set aside.**

Cook!

- **Place the milk in a 6- to 8-quart pan over medium heat, uncovered, and bring to a boil. This will take about 10 to 12 minutes. Watch it carefully so it does not boil over, and stir frequently to prevent scorching the milk.**
- **Add the drained rice. Return it to a boil. This will take 1 to 2 minutes.**
- **Reduce to a simmer and cook, uncovered, for 30 to 35 minutes. The rice will absorb the milk as it cooks and thickens. Stir frequently, occasionally mashing the rice with a whisk.**
- **If the rice sticks, lower the heat.**
- **After all the milk has been absorbed and the rice is very tender, add the sugar and cardamom. Stir well to combine all the ingredients.**
- **Pour the rice into a heat-proof bowl. Let it cool for 10 to 15 minutes, and then cover and chill completely.**
- **When ready to serve, spoon the chilled dessert into individual serving dishes and garnish each serving with the pistachios, raisins, and sliced almonds.**

Helpful Kitchen Equipment and Utensils

CUTTING BOARD

ASSORTED KNIVES

VEGETABLE PEELER

SAUCEPANS WITH LIDS

STOCKPOT WITH LID

SPATULA

WHISK

BAKING PAN

ELECTRIC MIXER

MIXING BOWL

LADLE

LARGE METAL SPOON

COOKIE SHEET

SMALL HAND STRAINER

FOUR-SIDED GRATER

COLANDER

JUICER

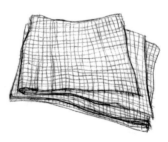

CHEESECLOTH

MORTAR AND PESTLE

FOOD PROCESSOR

BLENDER

COFFEE/SPICE GRINDER

ALLSPICE

This tiny berry comes from the West Indies. It is strongly aromatic, suggesting cloves with a hint of cinnamon and nutmeg. To receive the maximum flavor from these dark purple berries, it is best to buy them whole and grind them yourself.

CARDAMOM

Cardamom seed is taken from the dried fruit of a member of the ginger family. It is the third most expensive spice in the world after saffron and vanilla. Two types of these curious seeds are available. Black cardamom, with its dark and wrinkled pod or shell, is used in curries, soups, and stews. Green cardamom is used in desserts because of its sweet flavor. The hard outer pods must be removed to get to the seeds inside. You can buy cardamom already ground, though it is not as flavorful as the whole spice.

CHILE PEPPERS

Be very careful when you handle some varieties of chiles because they can be hot! When you cook with hot chiles, wear rubber gloves to protect your skin, and be very careful not to touch your eyes or mouth. Chile peppers can be used fresh or dried, and they add great flavor to a dish. Indian cooks use long green or red chiles to achieve an authentic taste, however, jalapeño and serrano peppers are excellent substitutes for all the recipes in this book and are available in supermarkets.

CILANTRO

Cilantro is an herb also known as fresh coriander or Chinese parsley. Cilantro is easily confused with parsley but has a bolder flavor and a spicy aroma. It should be washed to remove any dirt still clinging to the stems or leaves and then dried in paper towels. Wrap it in plastic and it will keep for about a week in the refrigerator.

CLOVES

A clove is the tiny dried flower bud of an evergreen tree. It is popular in Indian cooking for its flavor. It comes whole or ground. If you buy it whole and grind it yourself, you're assured of the best flavor. It should be used sparingly because cloves can easily overpower the other flavors in your recipe.

CORIANDER SEEDS

The fast-growing coriander plant, a member of the carrot family, produces seeds at the end of its growing cycle. Coriander seeds are very popular in Indian cooking. Noted for their lemony taste and sweet aroma, they add subtle flavor and a slight hint of pepper to many dishes. It is best to grind them as they are needed in order to achieve the maximum flavor. You can buy the seeds already ground, but the powder tends to have a bitter flavor, so if you use it, use a bit less of it than freshly ground.

CUMIN SEEDS

The cumin seed, a member of the parsley family, is a familiar spice in Indian cooking. It is used whole to flavor cooking oil or ground for use in spice mixes.

CURRY POWDER

This popular blend of spices and herbs is really a product of the United Kingdom and not India. Many years ago, several Indian spices were blended together by Indian cooks at the request of British subjects returning home. When they wanted a taste of India, they used this combination of spices to remind them of the pleasures of the native Indian cooking they had left behind.

FENNEL SEEDS

Fennel is a member of the parsley family. It is popular for its licorice flavor and slightly sweet aftertaste. It is used in many Indian recipes and is available whole or ground. It is sometimes lightly roasted to release its flavor before it is ground into a powder. Eating a fennel seed will sweeten your breath.

GARAM MASALA

Read more about garam masala on page 8 or follow the recipe on page 43 to make your own.

GARLIC

Garlic is a member of the onion family and a key ingredient to much of Indian cooking. When you purchase garlic, look for large bulbs that are hard and solid. The bulb is comprised of cloves. To use the cloves, first separate them from the bulb, then with the flat side of a knife, give them a good whack. Then remove the white paperlike skin and cut off the dark tip. The cloves can be chopped into small pieces, mashed, or cut into thin slices. Many nutritionists believe that garlic has great health benefits because it is rich in minerals.

GINGER

Ginger, sometimes called gingerroot, is really a rhizome. It is a very important spice in Indian cooking both in the north and the south. When you shop for fresh ginger, look for firm texture and a nice smooth skin with no dark spots. Peel off the outer skin with a vegetable peeler. Then slice off the amount the recipe calls for, using a sharp knife. Ginger will keep in the refrigerator for up to two weeks. You can use a garlic press to crush it. A grater or zester also works to get the juice out of it.

LENTILS

The lentil, or *dal* as it called in India, is a main ingredient in Indian dishes. It comes in red, yellow, gray, and even pink varieties. Lentils are packed with protein so India's huge vegetarian population relies on them as an essential part of their diet. It is important that you check dried lentils carefully to remove any stones or debris before cooking them. Dried lentils can be kept in an airtight container for a long time.

MUSTARD SEEDS

Mustard seeds have been used in cooking for thousands of years. The two common varieties are yellow and black. They are essential to Indian cooking, as they are used to flavor hot oils or are ground into spice mixes. Mustard seeds are used to make (what else?) mustard—one of the most popular condiments in the world.

NUTMEG

This spice is native to Indonesia. It gives dishes a warm, soft flavor. It is best to buy it whole and grate it only when you need some for your recipe. Store the nutmeg sealed in a glass jar, and it will keep a long time.

SAFFRON

Saffron is the most expensive spice in the world costing about $800 per pound. It comes from the crocus flower, and it takes 70,000 blooms to produce a single pound of the spice. Its color and flavor are essential in Indian cooking. The Moghuls used it in their cooking, and its influence is still evident in countless recipes in India today. Saffron is precious, so use it with great care and always return it to the container it was sold in. Never store it in direct sunlight.

TOMATOES

There is no doubt that tomatoes are a key ingredient to Indian cooking. When shopping for fresh tomatoes, look for a nice rich, red color and avoid the ones with spots or bruises. If you are unable to find good fresh tomatoes, don't hesitate to buy canned. To store fresh tomatoes, keep them away from heat, but never put them in the refrigerator; the cold will destroy their flavor and texture.

TURMERIC

India is the largest producer of turmeric in the world. A rhizome similar to ginger, turmeric is picked young, cleaned, boiled, then dried in the sun. It is then ground into a golden powder. Some say it is the soul of Indian cooking, as it is used in countless Indian dishes. But be careful! Turmeric will stain, and the stains are not easy to remove; that is probably why it is used as a fabric dye in India as well as a spice. It's a good idea to use a spoon when cooking with turmeric, so you will keep it on the food and not on you.

INDEX

METRIC CONVERSION CHART

You can use the chart below to convert from U.S. measurements to the metric system.

Weight
1 ounce = 28 grams
1/2 pound (8 ounces) = 227 grams
1 pound = .45 kilograms
2.2 pounds = 1 kilogram

Liquid volume
1 teaspoon = 5 milliliters
1 tablespoon = 15 milliliters
1 fluid ounce = 30 milliliters
1 cup = 240 milliliters (.24 liters)
1 pint = 480 milliliters (.48 liters)
1 quart = .95 liter

Length
1/4 inch = .6 centimeter
1/2 inch = 1.25 centimeters
1 inch = 2.5 centimeters

Temperature
100°F = 40°C
110°F = 45°C
212°F = 100°C (boiling point of water)
350°F = 180°C
375°F = 190°C
400°F = 200°C
425°F = 220°C
450°F = 235°C
(To convert temperatures in Fahrenheit to Celsius, subtract 32 and multiply by .56)